What Those People Need Is a Puppy!

More Cartoons by Pat Oliphant

Andrews and McMeel
A Universal Press Syndicate Company
Kansas City • New York

Oliphant® is syndicated internationally by Universal Press Syndicate.

What Those People Need Is a Puppy! copyright © 1989 by Universal Press Syndicate. All rights reserved. Printed in the United States of America. No part of this book may be used or reproduced in any manner whatsoever without written permission except in the case of reprints in the context of reviews. For information write Andrews and McMeel, a Universal Press Syndicate Company, 4900 Main Street, Kansas City, Missouri 64112.

ISBN: 0-8362-1857-4

Library of Congress Catalog Card Number: 89-84808

HIS RUNNING MATE

August 1, 1988

'I INTEND BEING A STRONG VICE-PRESIDENT, AN ALTERNATE OPINION AS YOU MIGHT SAY, NOT JUST A RUBBER STAMP LIKE GEORGE BUSH, BUT A FORCEFUL VOICE OF LOYAL DISSENT...'

'HOW MANY TIMES HAVE YOU BEEN TOLD NOT TO GO IN THE SEA? YOU KNOW YOUR DADDY'S MOB HAS THE DISPOSAL CONTRACT IN THIS AREA.'

August 9, 1988

8

August 9, 1988

`..AND NEXT WE CAN LOOK FORWARD TO THE GREENHOUSE EFFECT RAISING THE LEVEL OF THE WORLD'S OCEANS.´

9

THE LAST TEMPTATION OF RONALD REAGAN

'NO DRINKING, NO SMOKING, NO EATING MEAT, NO SUGAR, NO SALT, NO SUNSHINE, NO SEX —
I'LL BE DOWNSTAIRS BREATHING THE RADON.'

August 13, 1988

13

'BELIEVE ME, I'M MY OWN MAN, NOW — IF I MAKE THE EXECUTIVE DECISION TO CAMPAIGN WITH MY FOOT STUCK IN THIS, THEN THAT'S THE WAY IT'S GONNA BE.'

August 25, 1988

AND SO, IN A STRANGE CHAIN OF EVENTS, LITTLE DANFORTH SUDDENLY FOUND HIMSELF FORTY-SECOND PRESIDENT OF THE UNITED STATES.

17

August 25, 1988

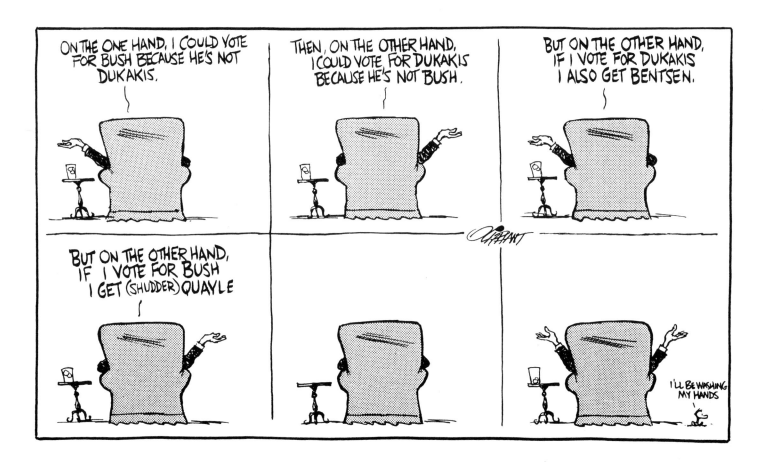

August 30, 1988

20

August 31, 1988

KNOWLEDGEABLE MAN OF GOVERNMENT,
EXPERIENCED SERVANT OF THE PEOPLE,
SOLDIER, STATESMAN,
FEARLESS PATRIOT,
DEFENDER OF THE PLEDGE OF ALLEGIANCE,
MORE-AMERICAN-THAN-THOU AND ALL-ROUND GOOD-GUY CANDIDATE,
HERE HE IS, YOUR PRESIDENT AND MINE,
MICHAEL BUSH
ACE ENGRAVIN
NEVER MIND - IF THEY STAY OFF THE ISSUES, NO-ONE WILL EVEN NOTICE

'AND HERE WE ARE AT THE BOTTOM OF BOSTON HARBOR, TALKING WITH GOVERNOR DUKAKIS ABOUT ENVIRONMENTAL CONCERNS...'

September 7, 1988

September 8, 1988

26

'WOW! GOLLY, SO IT IS! WELL, GOSH, IT'S BEEN YEARS! AND HOW ARE THINGS WITH YOU, DAD?'

'I PLEDGE ALLEGIANCE TO THE BAG, AND TO THE ELECTION-YEAR LEGISLATION WHICH IT CONTAINS...'

September 26, 1988

September 29, 1988

35

SECOND DEBATE.

'MEDIA FEEDING TIME — I LOVE IT!'

October 6, 1988

'SO MUCH FOR THE PLEBISCITE. WE'LL MANAGE THE GENERAL ELECTION MORE CAREFULLY.'

October 11, 1988

'HERE ARE THE NEW PRESIDENT'S FIRST INSTRUCTIONS: ICE CREAM AND PLENTY OF IT, TWENTY HAMBURGERS, LARGE FRIES AND TEN COKES. HE GETS TO STAY UP LATE AS HE LIKES, AND HE WANTS A PONY.'

43

October 12, 1988

44

October 13, 1988

'NO ONE CAN SAVE YOU, MY DEAR—THERE AIN'T NO HEROES ANY MORE!'

46

October 17, 1988

'OK, YOU'VE GOT HIM WORRIED — THE TRICK NOW IS NOT TO APPEAR OVER-CONFIDENT.'

47

October 19, 1988

'SEND ALL THE DRESSES BACK!? CAN'T I KEEP JUST <u>ONE</u>??'

October 20, 1988

GEORGE BUSH AND MICHAEL DUKAKIS SHARE THE 1988 NOBEL PIES FOR SORRY POLITICAL CAMPAIGNING.

49

October 20, 1988

'GREETINGS. WE ARE FROM THE GOVERNMENT. WE ARE HERE TO HELP YOU.'

50

October 24, 1988

October 25, 1988

October 26, 1988

THE GHOSTS OF HALLOWEEN HOUSE.

53

November 1, 1988

A CARTOONIST'S PRAYER.

THE VOTER WHO COULDN'T REMEMBER.

November 7, 1988

'A VIRUS JUST ATE THE ENTIRE VOTE COUNT — WE'LL HAVE TO HOLD THE ELECTION OVER AGAIN!'

November 9, 1988

62

November 11, 1988

63

November 14, 1988

November 15, 1988

'MEIN GOLLY — I HOPE GEORGE BUSH VON'T CRITICIZE ME FOR ALLOWING MEINSELF TO BE CARRIED AVAY BY SOME SCREWY, RIGHT-VING FUNDAMENTALISTS!'

65

'IN THE BOTTLES, PLEASE, GENTLEMEN!'

November 17, 1988

67

November 18, 1988

'WADDAYA MEAN, WASTE??! THIS AIRCRAFT IS A HIGHLY SUCCESSFUL TEST VEHICLE FOR A PERFECTLY FUNCTIONING EJECTION SEAT SYSTEM!'

November 29, 1988

`SIR, THE BEAR IS LOOSE...`

December 7, 1988

'GIVE HIM A CABINET POSITION. MAKE HIM SECRETARY FOR GOLF — HE'S YOUR VICE PRESIDENT.'

December 8, 1988

December 12, 1988

79

'LOOK AT ALL THAT TERRIBLE DEVASTATION IN ARMENIA, MOMMY... IT SURE MAKES ME FEEL PROUD TO BE AN ANTI-COMMUNIST.'

December 15, 1988

82

A REAGANVILLE CHRISTMAS.

THE IRON TRIANGLE

December 20, 1988

'AND NOW, FOR THOSE OF YOU WHO THOUGHT TERRORISM WAS A THING OF THE PAST...'

December 21, 1988

'THIS WOULDN'T BE HAPPENING IF WE WERE A SAVINGS AND LOAN.'

LET THE HONEYMOON COMMENCE.

January 5, 1989

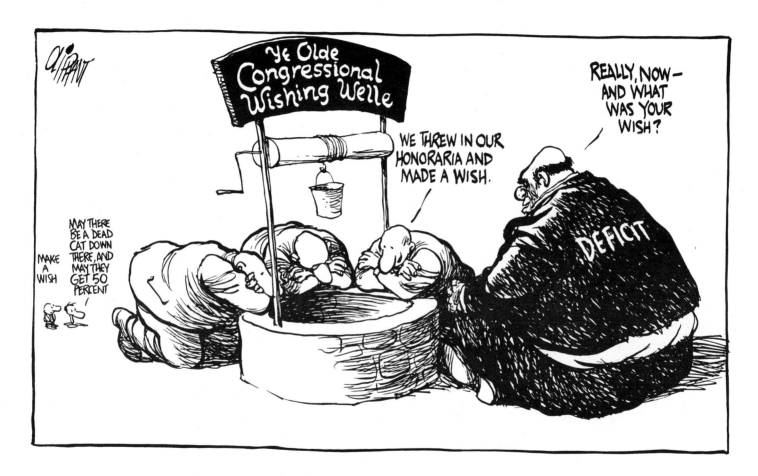

92

January 9, 1989

'Perhaps ve could interest you in Global Supremacy through Pharmaceutical Investment, ja?'

94

'TO MY DEAR NEPHEW, GEORGE, I LEAVE MY LITTLE PUPPY DOG...'

January 11, 1989

January 12, 1989

REAGAN'S REGIMENT: THE COMMANDER-IN-CHIEF REVIEWS THE TROOPS FOR THE LAST TIME.

97

January 12, 1989

January 18, 1989

101

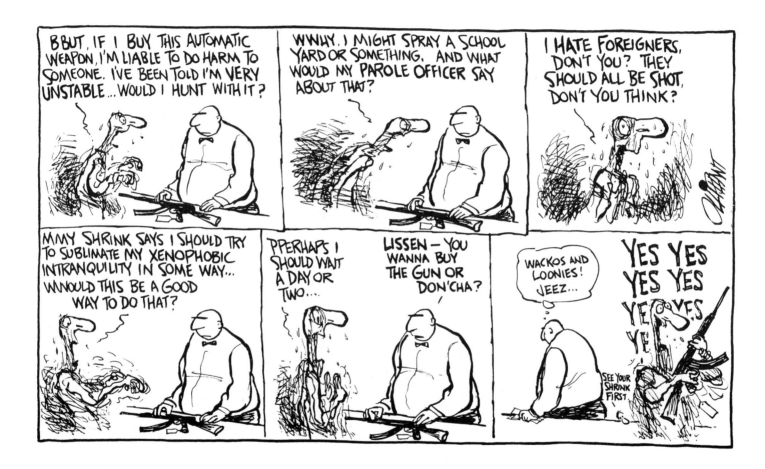

MEANWHILE, DEEP IN THE WHITE HOUSE BASEMENT, A LONELY HOSTAGE AWAITS RESCUE...

'I ADORE THE BUSH STYLE, BUT I THINK IT LOOKS BETTER ON BARBARA.'

January 25, 1989

IF IT <u>LOOKS</u> LIKE A DUCK...

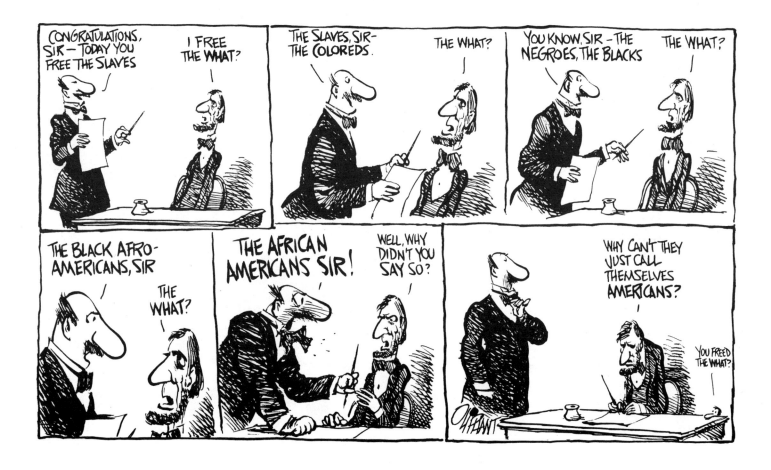

Deportment of Eddercation
Sers. Wuns mor you hav plased a sler up on the nashens teenaggers with anothar of yor roten serveys and make us look like iggeramuses. Before you have say we ar no good at geogerfy or history or speling now it is math and sience we ar no good at too also you say. Enuf i say Enny mor of this and i will buy a gun and shoot up the skool. That wood tich you a lessen. yor frend Robert Nokkdonger III ag 16
WHERE DID YOU GET A WORD LIKE IGGERAMUS?
OLIPHANT

'SORRY, PAL — JUDGE GESELL SAYS IF YOU NEVER HEARD OF OLLIE NORTH, YOU GOT JURY DUTY.'

113

February 6, 1989

'THANK YOU— THERE WILL ALSO BE A SURCHARGE FOR BEGGING AND RECOVERY FEES, CUP RENTAL AND VARIOUS MISMANAGEMENT COSTS WHICH WE MUST PASS ALONG TO THE CUSTOMER.'

'AND WHICH OF US DIDN'T CHECK OUR GUN BEFORE CLASS?'

February 14, 1989

119

February 15, 1989

THE APPEARANCE OF ETHICS — BEATIFICATION OF THE BLESSED JAMES A. BAKER III.

'IN THE OPINION OF THIS REVIEWER...'

February 17, 1989

AN AMERICAN EDUCATION. (CONTINUED)

122

'A MR. SALMAN RUSHDIE. HE HAS AN IDEA FOR A BOOK.'

February 22, 1989

124

'GOODNESS! AND YOU SAY I CAN ALSO HUNT WITH IT?'

February 27, 1989

126

March 3, 1989

`SENATOR TOWER? WHY, NO, YOU JUST MISSED HIM

March 6, 1989

131

March 7, 1989

'BURN THEM? YOU MEAN ALL OF THEM?'

March 8, 1989

133

March 9, 1989

THE SENATE HANDS JOHN TOWER HIS HAT...

AND PRESIDENT BUSH HIS PURSE.

THE GLORY AND THE POWER.

March 14, 1989

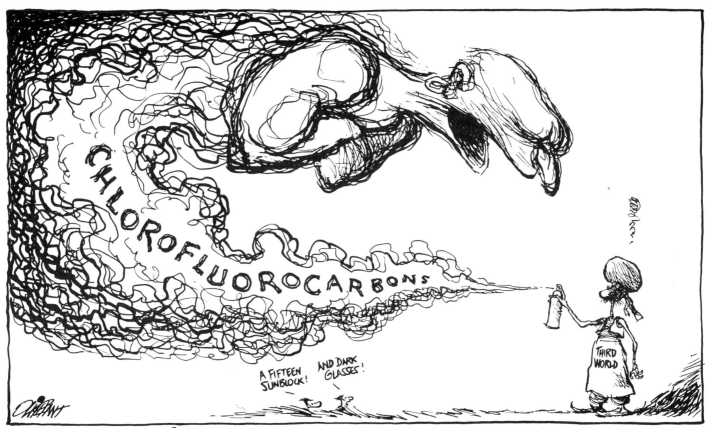

'BEFORE I KILL YOU, DO YOU HAVE ANY OTHER WISHES?'

137

March 16, 1989

'NOW MAYBE YOU UNDERSTAND WHY I NEED AN ASSAULT RIFLE — BECAUSE THEY'RE COMIN' TO TAKE IT AWAY, IS WHY.'

March 20, 1989

CALIFORNIA TAKES THE BULL BY THE HORNS

141

March 22, 1989

UNINDICTED CO·CONSPIRATORS.

MR. MICHEL, YOUR DOG IS LOOSE!

March 24, 1989

"TELL YOU HOW I VOTED?? WHY, I THOUGHT THAT SORT OF INTRUSIVE MEDDLING WITH THE DEMOCRATIC PROCESS ONLY HAPPENED IN AMERICA!"

144

March 27, 1989

'OOPS—SOMEBODY SHOULD CLEAN THAT UP!'

March 31, 1989

MEMO ALL EXXON EXECUTIVES: THE CEO HAS PROMISED TO CLEAN UP. PLEASE REPORT TO THE BEACH.

April 1, 1989

HONOR AMONG STOOL PIGEONS AND OTHERS.

April 4, 1989

THE CASE **FOR** SEMI-AUTOMATIC ASSAULT WEAPONS.

'OH, THE HECK WITH IT — I'D RATHER BE THE EDUCATION PRESIDENT.'

April 10, 1989

'JUST SIGN HERE TO DECLARE YOU'RE NOT A CERTIFIABLE CRAZY.'

April 11, 1989

156

April 12, 1989

157

A CAUCUS OF DEMOCRATS.

April 20, 1989

'YOU'RE FREE TO GO, MR. S&L, SIR — WE CAUGHT THE REAL FELON.'

April 24, 1989

RIP VAN BUSH, THE MAN WHO SLEPT FOR 100 DAYS...

April 27, 1989

'THE PRO-LIFERS SENT ME.'

163

June 12, 1989

CORPORATE CHESS.

June 26, 1989

June 28, 1989

June 30, 1989

173

July 7, 1989

'I GOT A GREAT IDEA, GENERAL BENNETT— WHENEVER WE SEIZE DRUGS, WE RESELL THE DRUGS AND WE USE THE MONEY TO FINANCE THE WAR ON DRUGS.'

175

July 10, 1989

'I SUPPOSE WE MUST ACCEPT THAT THE REVEREND STALLINGS HEARS A DIFFERENT DRUMMER.'